mindfulness, meditation and opening the the third eye

Table of Contents

1 Introduction to Mindfulness and Meditation

2 Exploring the Third Eye

3 Ancient Wisdom and Modern Science

4 Mindfulness in Daily Life

5 Meditation Techniques

Introduction to Mindfulness and Meditation

Understanding Mindfulness

Mindfulness is a concept that has gained popularity in recent years due to its remarkable benefits in daily life. It is the practice of being fully present in the current moment and paying attention to your thoughts, feelings, and sensations without judgment. In today's fast-paced and stressful world, it can be challenging to stay centered and focused on the present. However, incorporating mindfulness into your daily routine can have a transformative effect on your well-being.

One of the key aspects of mindfulness is being aware of the present moment. It involves bringing your attention to the here and now, rather than dwelling on the past or worrying about the future. By doing so, you cultivate a sense of clarity and focus, allowing you to fully experience each moment of your life.

The benefits of practicing mindfulness are widespread and have been scientifically proven. Research has shown that regular mindfulness practice can reduce stress and anxiety levels, improve cognitive function, enhance emotional well-being, and even strengthen the immune system. By developing mindfulness, you create a space within yourself that allows you to respond to life's challenges with a greater sense of calmness and resilience.

There are various techniques and exercises that can help you cultivate mindfulness. One commonly used technique is mindful breathing, which involves paying attention to your breath as it moves in and out of your body. This simple practice helps anchor your attention to the present moment and increases your awareness of your body and mind.

Another technique is body scan meditation, where you systematically focus on different parts of your body, from head to toe, and notice any physical sensations or tensions. This practice promotes a sense of relaxation and body awareness.

Mindful walking is also a powerful exercise that can be incorporated into your daily routine. It involves walking slowly and deliberately, paying attention to each step, the sensation of your feet touching the ground, and the movement of your body. This practice not only helps you connect with your environment but also brings a sense of grounding and stability.

These are just a few examples of the many techniques available to cultivate mindfulness. By exploring and incorporating these practices into your life, you can experience the profound benefits of mindfulness and create a greater sense of well-being.

The Benefits of Meditation

{{subchapter}}: The Benefits of Meditation

When it comes to promoting overall well-being, meditation has gained significant recognition in recent years. This ancient practice offers numerous benefits for the mind, body, and spirit. Let's explore some of the positive effects of meditation and how it can enhance your life.

Mental Health:

Regular meditation has been shown to have a positive impact on mental health. It can help reduce stress, anxiety, and even symptoms of depression. By practicing mindfulness in meditation, you can learn to focus your attention on the present moment, allowing stressful thoughts and worries to fade away. This leads to improved mental clarity and a greater sense of inner peace.

Emotional Well-being:

Meditation also has profound effects on emotional well-being. It can help regulate emotions, increase self-awareness, and promote a positive outlook on life. By cultivating a mindful and non-judgmental attitude, you can develop better emotional intelligence and cope more effectively with challenging situations. This ultimately leads to increased happiness and a greater sense of fulfillment in life.

Physical Health:

It's not just the mind and emotions that benefit from meditation â€" the body also reaps rewards. Research has shown that regular meditation can lower blood pressure, reduce the risk of heart disease, and even strengthen the immune system. By reducing stress levels, meditation also helps alleviate chronic pain and promotes better sleep, resulting in improved overall physical health.

The Science Behind Meditation:

Scientific studies have provided evidence supporting the benefits of meditation. Brain imaging studies have shown that regular meditation can increase brain activity in regions associated with focus, attention, and emotional regulation. These changes in brain structure can lead to improved cognitive function, increased creativity, and enhanced memory.

Enhancing Focus and Concentration:

For those seeking to sharpen their focus and concentration, meditation is a powerful tool. By practicing mindfulness meditation, you can train your mind to remain present and fully engaged in whatever task you are performing. This skill translates into improved productivity, better decision-making, and increased effectiveness in both personal and professional pursuits.

Cultivating Mindfulness:

Meditation is the gateway to mindfulness â€" the state of being fully aware and present in the moment. Mindfulness brings about a sense of deep peace and contentment. By incorporating meditation into your daily routine, you can develop and strengthen this state of mindfulness, allowing you to experience life more fully and joyfully.

Conclusion:

The benefits of meditation are far-reaching and have been scientifically proven. By embracing this ancient practice, you can enhance your mental, emotional, and physical well-being. Through regular meditation, you will cultivate mindfulness, improve focus and concentration, and foster a greater sense of peace and happiness in your life.

Different Types of Meditation

In this section, we will explore different types of meditation practices that are followed by various cultures around the world. Meditation has been an integral part of spiritual traditions and is known for its ability to cultivate inner peace, mindfulness, and self-awareness. By learning about these different meditation techniques, you can explore which one resonates with you the most and incorporate it into your daily spiritual practice.

1. Mindfulness Meditation:

Mindfulness meditation is a practice that involves focusing your attention on the present moment without judgment. It stems from Buddhist traditions but has gained popularity in recent years due to its effectiveness in reducing stress and enhancing overall well-being. With mindfulness meditation, you develop the ability to observe your thoughts, emotions, and bodily sensations without engaging or reacting to them. It allows you to cultivate a sense of calmness and equanimity.

2. Loving-Kindness Meditation:

Loving-kindness meditation, also known as metta meditation, is a practice rooted in the teachings of Buddhism. It involves directing feelings of love, compassion, and goodwill towards oneself and others. By cultivating feelings of love and kindness, you cultivate empathy and develop a more positive outlook towards yourself and others. This practice helps in creating harmony within and fosters a sense of connection with all beings.

3. Body Scan Meditation:

Body scan meditation is a technique that involves systematically scanning your body from head to toe, bringing attention to all the physical sensations and tensions you may be experiencing. This practice helps in developing a deeper connection with your body and increasing body awareness. By bringing attention to different parts of the body, you learn to notice and release any areas of tension or discomfort, promoting relaxation and overall well-being.

Each type of meditation practice offers unique benefits and features:

- Mindfulness meditation increases self-awareness, reduces stress, and promotes equanimity.
- Loving-kindness meditation cultivates compassion, empathy, and a positive mindset.
- Body scan meditation enhances body awareness, promotes relaxation, and aids in releasing tension.

By exploring these different meditation practices, you can choose the one that resonates with you the most and incorporate it into your spiritual journey. Remember, it's important to approach meditation with an open mind and give each practice a fair chance to experience its benefits fully.

Exploring the Third Eye

The Concept of the Third Eye

The third eye is a concept that has captured the interest and curiosity of many spiritual seekers throughout history. It is often associated with intuition, inner knowing, and spiritual awakening. In this subchapter, we will explore the concept of the third eye and its significance in various spiritual traditions.

Throughout different cultures and belief systems, the third eye is often depicted as an inner eye or a symbol of higher consciousness. It is said to provide a deeper insight and understanding of the world beyond what our physical senses can perceive.

According to ancient Indian spiritual traditions, the third eye, also known as the Ajna chakra, is located in the center of the forehead, between the eyebrows. It is considered the seat of intuition and the gateway to higher states of consciousness. In Hinduism, the third eye is associated with Lord Shiva, the deity of destruction and transformation.

In Buddhism, the third eye is referred to as the urna and is represented as a small circular mark on the forehead, often seen on statues of the Buddha. It signifies wisdom and insight, and is believed to help practitioners see beyond the illusions of the material world.

In ancient Egyptian mythology, the eye of Horus, also known as the Wedjat eye, symbolizes protection, healing, and intuition. It was believed to grant the wearer spiritual vision and the ability to connect with the divine.

The third eye is not only associated with higher consciousness, but also with personal transformation and spiritual awakening. It is believed to open up a realm of expanded awareness, allowing individuals to tap into their inner wisdom and access higher realms of consciousness.

Many spiritual practices, such as meditation, visualization, and energy healing, focus on activating and awakening the third eye. By working with the energy of this chakra, individuals can enhance their intuition, gain clarity and insight, and develop a deeper connection with their higher self.

In conclusion, the concept of the third eye holds great significance in various spiritual traditions. It represents our innate ability to access higher levels of consciousness and perceive the world beyond our physical senses. By awakening and activating our third eye, we can tap into our intuition, gain deeper insights, and embark on a journey of spiritual awakening and self-discovery.

Opening and Activating the Third Eye

Opening and activating the third eye is a practice that has been embraced and explored by many spiritual seekers in the New Age community. It is believed to enhance intuition, expand consciousness, and provide a deeper connection to the spiritual realm.

There are various techniques and practices that can assist in opening and activating the third eye. These practices aim to stimulate and awaken the pineal gland, which is considered the physical counterpart to the third eye in the human body.

One effective technique is meditation. By quieting the mind and focusing on the third eye area, individuals can create a space for the energy to flow freely. This can be achieved through techniques such as breathwork and visualization.

Another practice that can enhance third eye activation is energy work. This involves working with subtle energy to balance and align the chakras, with specific attention to the third eye chakra, also known as the Ajna chakra. Energy healing modalities such as Reiki and crystal healing can be beneficial in this process.

Intention is key when it comes to opening and activating the third eye. By setting a clear and focused intention to awaken this spiritual center, individuals can harness their energy and direct it towards the third eye. This intention acts as a catalyst for the awakening process.

Visualization is a powerful tool in third eye activation. By visualizing the third eye as an open and vibrant energy center, individuals can strengthen their connection to it. Visualizing a bright indigo light at the center of the forehead can help to activate and energize the third eye.

It is important to approach the practice of opening and activating the third eye with patience and self-care. Results may vary for each individual, and it is crucial to listen to your own intuition and proceed at a pace that feels comfortable for you.

With regular practice and dedication, the third eye can be awakened and activated, leading to a heightened sense of awareness and a deeper connection to the spiritual realm.

Exercises and Practices for Third Eye Awakening

Are you ready to enhance your third eye perception and intuition? In this section, we will explore a variety of exercises and practices that can help awaken and strengthen your third eye. Through consistent practice, you can expand your consciousness and tap into your intuitive abilities in profound ways.

1. Meditation: Meditation is a powerful tool for opening and activating the third eye. Find a quiet and comfortable space, close your eyes, and focus your attention on the space between your eyebrows. Visualize a vibrant indigo light radiating from this area, and allow yourself to enter a deep state of relaxation. Regular meditation practice can help you attune to the subtle energies of the third eye and increase your overall intuitive awareness.

2. Visualization: Visualization exercises can help stimulate the third eye and enhance your ability to visualize with clarity. Choose an object or symbol that resonates with you, and visualize it in vivid detail. Imagine the object rotating, expanding, or changing colors. As you practice, your visualization skills will improve, and you'll develop a greater capacity to receive intuitive insights through imagery.

3. Breathwork: Conscious breathing techniques can assist in balancing and energizing the third eye. One simple practice involves inhaling deeply through your nose, imagining the breath flowing up through your spine and into your third eye, and then exhaling slowly through your mouth. You can also experiment with alternate nostril breathing for an additional balancing effect.

4. Journaling: Keeping a journal can be a valuable tool for recording your intuitive experiences and insights. Set aside a few minutes each day to write about your dreams, synchronicities, and any intuitive impressions you may receive. By consistently documenting your experiences, you can begin to recognize patterns and gain a deeper understanding of your own intuitive abilities.

5. Intuitive Exercises: Engage in activities that encourage you to trust your intuition and make intuitive decisions. For example, when faced with a choice, take a moment to close your eyes, tune into your inner guidance, and follow the guidance that arises. This practice strengthens your connection to your intuition and helps you become more attuned to the subtle messages of your third eye.

Remember, awakening the third eye is a gradual process that requires dedication and patience. Be consistent with your practice, and allow yourself to remain open to the journey of self-discovery and expanded consciousness.

Ancient Wisdom and Modern Science

Historical Origins of Mindfulness and Meditation

Tracing the historical origins of mindfulness and meditation is fascinating, as these practices have deep roots in ancient cultures and spiritual traditions. Let's dive into the rich history of mindfulness and meditation to understand how they have evolved over time.

Ancient cultures across the world have long recognized the benefits of mindfulness and meditation. In ancient India, these practices were an integral part of spiritual traditions and were documented in ancient texts like the Vedas and Upanishads. These texts provided insights into the techniques and philosophies behind mindfulness and meditation.

Gautama Buddha, often considered the founder of Buddhism, played a crucial role in the development and popularization of mindfulness and meditation. Buddha's teachings emphasized the practice of meditation as a means to achieve enlightenment. His teachings spread across Asia, leading to the establishment of Buddhist traditions that further refined and expanded these practices.

The transmission of mindfulness and meditation practices throughout history has been influenced by various factors. During the spread of Buddhism, these practices were disseminated through monastic communities and traveled along ancient trade routes. The incorporation of mindfulness and meditation in Taoist and Confucian traditions in China also contributed to their diffusion.

In the 20th century, the popularity of mindfulness and meditation practices expanded beyond their traditional roots. Influential figures like Thich Nhat Hanh and Jon Kabat-Zinn introduced mindfulness practices to the West, adapting and integrating them into secular contexts. These adaptations formed the basis for the modern practice of mindfulness that we see today.

Mindfulness and meditation have come a long way from their ancient origins, and their benefits are now widely recognized by individuals seeking personal growth and well-being. The practice of mindfulness and meditation continues to evolve and adapt to the needs of contemporary society, demonstrating the timeless relevance of these ancient traditions.

Scientific Studies on Mindfulness and Meditation

Scientific Studies on Mindfulness and Meditation

In recent years, there has been a surge of interest in studying the effects of mindfulness and meditation on various aspects of human well-being. Researchers from around the world have conducted a multitude of scientific studies to better understand the potential benefits of these practices. Let's explore some of the key findings from these studies.

1. Stress Reduction: Numerous studies have shown that mindfulness and meditation can help reduce stress levels. One study published in the Journal of Consulting and Clinical Psychology found that an eight-week mindfulness-based stress reduction program significantly decreased participants' levels of stress and anxiety. Another study conducted at Stanford University showed that individuals who regularly practiced meditation exhibited lower levels of the stress hormone cortisol.

2. Improved Brain Function: Research has revealed that mindfulness and meditation can have a positive impact on brain structure and cognitive function. A study published in the journal NeuroImage found that long-term meditation practitioners had increased gray matter volume in brain regions associated with attention, sensory perception, and emotional regulation. Additionally, a review of several studies conducted by Harvard Medical School showed that mindfulness meditation can enhance attention and memory, as well as improve decision-making skills.

3. Emotional Well-being: Many studies have explored the effects of mindfulness and meditation on emotional well-being. Research conducted at the University of Wisconsin-Madison revealed that mindfulness meditation can increase activity in brain regions associated with positive emotions and decrease activity in regions associated with negative emotions. Furthermore, a study published in the Journal of Happiness Studies demonstrated that individuals who regularly practiced meditation reported higher levels of life satisfaction and happiness.

4. Physical Health: Besides mental well-being, mindfulness and meditation have also been linked to various physical health benefits. For example, a study published in the Journal of Alternative and Complementary Medicine found that mindfulness meditation can lower blood pressure and reduce the risk of cardiovascular diseases. Additionally, researchers from the University of California, Davis discovered that meditators had stronger immune system responses compared to non-meditators.

These studies and many others provide strong evidence for the positive effects of mindfulness and meditation on various aspects of human life. As more research is conducted, scientists are gaining a deeper understanding of these practices and their potential to enhance overall well-being. The growing interest and recognition of mindfulness and meditation in the scientific community further emphasizes the importance of incorporating these practices into our daily lives.

Integration of Eastern and Western Practices

Eastern mindfulness and meditation practices have been integrated into Western psychology and healthcare with the aim of providing holistic approaches to mental and physical well-being. This integration has allowed individuals in the Western world to access ancient mindfulness and meditation techniques that were traditionally associated with Eastern philosophies and religions.

One of the key aspects of integrating Eastern and Western practices is the understanding that mindfulness and meditation can be utilized as tools for self-reflection, stress reduction, and overall mental health improvement. Western psychology and healthcare practitioners have recognized the benefits of incorporating these practices into their treatment approaches, and as a result, mindfulness-based therapies and interventions have gained popularity.

One of the most well-known mindfulness-based therapies is Mindfulness-Based Stress Reduction (MBSR), which was developed by Jon Kabat-Zinn in the late 1970s. This therapy combines elements of Eastern meditation practices, such as mindfulness meditation and body scan meditation, with Western psychological techniques. MBSR has been widely adopted in Western healthcare settings and has shown promising results in reducing stress, anxiety, and improving overall well-being.

In addition to MBSR, mindfulness-based cognitive therapy (MBCT) has also emerged as a prominent approach in the integration of Eastern and Western practices. MBCT combines cognitive therapy techniques with mindfulness exercises to help individuals who suffer from recurrent depression or anxiety. It has been found to be effective in preventing relapses and promoting emotional well-being.

The integration of Eastern and Western practices in mindfulness and meditation has also created opportunities for individuals to explore their spirituality in a new age context. The merging of these practices allows individuals to develop a deeper understanding of themselves and their place in the world.

While the integration of Eastern mindfulness and meditation practices into Western psychology and healthcare has been generally well-received, it is not without its challenges. One of the challenges is the potential for misinterpretation and cultural appropriation. It is important for practitioners to approach these practices with respect and understanding of their origins to avoid diluting their true essence.

Furthermore, the adaptation of these practices to fit within the Western context sometimes requires a modification of traditional techniques. This can lead to debates about the authenticity of the practices and their effectiveness in achieving the desired outcomes.

Despite these challenges, the integration of Eastern mindfulness and meditation practices into Western psychology and healthcare has brought about numerous benefits. It has provided individuals with alternative approaches to managing their mental and physical well-being and has opened up new avenues for spiritual exploration. As the field continues to evolve, it is important for practitioners and researchers to work together to ensure the responsible integration of these practices into Western approaches.

Mindfulness in Daily Life

Applying Mindfulness to Relationships

When it comes to cultivating healthy and meaningful relationships, mindfulness can play a crucial role. Mindfulness is a practice that involves bringing one's attention to the present moment, with an attitude of openness and acceptance. By applying mindfulness to our relationships, we can enhance our connection with others and foster deeper understanding and empathy.

One of the key aspects of applying mindfulness to relationships is being fully present in our interactions. This means giving our full attention to the person we are with, without being distracted by our own thoughts or judgments. By doing so, we can better understand their perspective and respond in a more thoughtful and compassionate way.

Another important aspect of mindfulness in relationships is cultivating awareness of our own emotions and reactions. By developing this awareness, we can better manage our emotions during conflicts or disagreements, and respond in a more constructive manner. This can help to prevent unnecessary arguments and foster a more harmonious and loving connection.

In addition to being present and aware, mindfulness can also enhance our communication skills. By practicing active listening, we can truly hear and understand what the other person is saying, rather than just waiting for our turn to speak. This can create a safe and supportive space for open and honest communication, allowing both parties to feel heard and valued.

Furthermore, mindfulness can be helpful in conflict resolution. By approaching conflicts with an open mind and a non-judgmental attitude, we can explore creative solutions and find common ground. Instead of getting caught up in blame or defensiveness, mindfulness allows us to approach conflicts with empathy and understanding, resulting in more peaceful resolutions.

Another benefit of mindfulness in relationships is the development of emotional intelligence. Mindfulness helps us to tune into our own emotions and recognize them without judgment, which in turn gives us greater insight into the emotions of others. This heightened emotional intelligence allows us to respond to others with empathy and compassion, strengthening our relationships and fostering a deeper connection.

In conclusion, applying mindfulness to our relationships can have a profound impact on our connections with others. By being present, aware, and compassionate, we can enhance our communication skills, resolve conflicts more effectively, and develop stronger emotional intelligence. By incorporating mindfulness into our daily interactions, we can cultivate healthy and meaningful relationships that bring joy and fulfillment into our lives.

Mindful Eating and Nutrition

Mindful eating is a concept that has gained much attention in recent years, and for good reason. It involves paying full attention to the experience of eating, from the preparation of the food to the act of consuming it. By engaging in mindful eating, individuals can develop a better understanding of their body's needs and cultivate a healthier relationship with food.

When it comes to nutrition, mindful eating can have a profound impact. It allows individuals to become more aware of the nutritional content of the foods they choose, leading to better overall health and well-being. By practicing mindful eating, individuals can make more conscious food choices and ensure they are receiving the necessary nutrients for optimal health.

One of the key aspects of mindful eating is mindful meal planning. This involves taking the time to plan out meals and snacks in advance, considering both taste and nutritional value. It is important to pay attention to food choices and select a variety of nutrient-dense foods to support overall health. By being mindful of food choices, individuals can ensure they are nourishing their body with the essential vitamins, minerals, and macronutrients it needs.

Practicing mindful eating can be a transformative experience. It allows individuals to savor and enjoy each bite, turning mealtime into a moment of pleasure and gratitude. By bringing awareness to the senses during the act of eating, individuals can enhance their enjoyment and satisfaction with food.

Here are some tips and techniques for practicing mindful eating:

1. Slow down and savor each bite.
2. Pay attention to the flavors, textures, and smells of the food.
3. Eat without distractions, such as television or smartphones.
4. Listen to your body's hunger and fullness cues.
5. Engage in mindful meal planning to ensure a variety of nutrient-dense foods.
6. Practice gratitude for the food you are consuming.

By incorporating mindful eating into your daily life, you can improve your relationship with food and enhance your overall health and well-being. Start practicing mindfulness today and experience the transformative power of mindful eating.

Mindfulness in Work and Productivity

Mindfulness, the practice of focusing one's attention on the present moment without judgment, has gained increasing popularity in recent years. And for good reason – the benefits of mindfulness in the workplace are numerous, particularly when it comes to reducing stress and improving focus. When individuals cultivate a mindful mindset, they are better equipped to handle the various stressors that arise in the workplace, leading to increased resilience and overall well-being.

One of the key advantages of mindfulness in the workplace is its ability to reduce stress. By bringing attention to the present moment, individuals can become aware of their thoughts, emotions, and physical sensations in a nonjudgmental way. This heightened self-awareness allows employees to recognize and respond to stressors more effectively, reducing the negative impact of stress on their mental and physical health. Moreover, practicing mindfulness can help individuals develop a greater sense of calm and equanimity, creating a more harmonious work environment.

Improved focus is another noteworthy benefit of incorporating mindfulness into the workplace. In today's fast-paced and technology-dependent world, it's easy to become distracted and scattered in our thoughts. However, by engaging in mindfulness practices, employees can sharpen their attention and concentration skills. Mindfulness helps individuals become more present and attentive, enabling them to stay focused on the task at hand amidst potential distractions, leading to enhanced productivity and efficiency.

If you're interested in incorporating mindfulness into your daily work routines and tasks, there are several techniques you can try. One effective approach is to start your day with a mindful morning ritual. This could involve taking a few moments to sit quietly and focus on your breath, setting an intention for the day, or engaging in a brief meditation practice. By starting the day in a mindful state, you can cultivate a sense of groundedness and set a positive tone for the rest of your workday.

Another technique is to practice mindful breaks throughout the day. Instead of mindlessly scrolling through your phone or reaching for a snack, take a few minutes to engage in a mindful activity. This could be as simple as going for a short walk outside, practicing deep breathing exercises, or doing a quick body scan to bring awareness to any tension or discomfort. These mindful breaks can help refresh your mind, increase your productivity, and reduce the risk of burnout.

In addition, integrating mindfulness into your work tasks can be beneficial. For example, you can approach each task with a sense of mindfulness by bringing your full attention and awareness to the present moment. Focus on one task at a time, minimizing multitasking, and practice deep engagement with the task at hand. By doing so, you can enhance your concentration, clarity, and overall performance.

Mindful productivity is a concept that explores how mindfulness practices can enhance not only our work performance but also our overall well-being and satisfaction in life. It goes beyond simply being productive and efficient; it emphasizes the importance of being present, purposeful, and balanced in our approach to work.

By integrating mindfulness into our work lives, we can cultivate a healthier work-life balance. Mindfulness practices can help us establish boundaries between work and personal life, allowing us to be fully present and engaged in both domains. Through mindful time management and prioritization, we can create a more harmonious and fulfilling lifestyle, reducing the risk of burnout and promoting overall well-being.

Mindful productivity also has a positive impact on job satisfaction. When we approach our work with mindfulness, we are more likely to find intrinsic fulfillment in our tasks, leading to greater job satisfaction. Mindfulness enables us to appreciate the present moment, celebrate small accomplishments, and find meaning in our work, even during challenging times. This sense of fulfillment and satisfaction can contribute to long-term career success and overall life satisfaction.

Meditation Techniques

Breath Awareness Meditation

Breath awareness meditation is a powerful technique that can bring calmness and grounding to our lives. By focusing on the breath, we can access a deeper state of relaxation and awareness. Whether you are new to meditation or have some experience, breath awareness meditation is a valuable practice that can help you cultivate a sense of inner peace and tranquility.

In this subchapter, we will explore the practice of breath awareness meditation and its many benefits.

When it comes to breath awareness meditation, there are several techniques that can be utilized to enhance your practice. One such technique is diaphragmatic breathing, also known as deep belly breathing. This technique involves breathing deeply into your diaphragm, allowing your abdomen to expand as you inhale and contract as you exhale. Diaphragmatic breathing promotes relaxation and helps to reduce stress and anxiety.

Another technique to explore is alternate nostril breathing. This technique involves using your thumb and finger to alternate the blocking of your nostrils while you breathe. By alternating the breath between the left and right nostrils, you can bring balance to both hemispheres of the brain and promote a sense of calm and focus.

These are just a few examples of the many breath-focused techniques that can be incorporated into your breath awareness meditation practice. Feel free to explore different techniques and find what resonates best with you.

If you are new to breath awareness meditation, it can be helpful to start with some guided instructions. Find a quiet and comfortable space where you can sit or lie down. Close your eyes and take a few deep breaths to relax your body and mind.

Once you are settled, bring your attention to your breath. Notice the sensation of the breath as you inhale and exhale. You can focus on the rising and falling of your abdomen or the feeling of the breath entering and leaving your nostrils. Simply observe the breath without trying to change it in any way.

If your mind starts to wander, gently bring your attention back to the breath. It's normal for thoughts to arise, but try not to get caught up in them. Just acknowledge them and let them go, returning your focus to the breath.

As you continue with your practice, you can progressively deepen your breath awareness meditation by gradually lengthening your inhales and exhales. This can help you to cultivate a deeper sense of relaxation and presence. You can also experiment with incorporating visualizations or affirmations into your practice for further enhancement.

Remember, breath awareness meditation is a practice, and it takes time and patience to fully reap its benefits. Be gentle with yourself as you explore and deepen your practice, and enjoy the journey of self-discovery and inner peace it brings.

Loving-Kindness Meditation

Loving-kindness meditation is a practice that cultivates compassion and empathy. It has long been used by spiritual seekers in the New Age community to foster a sense of love and understanding towards oneself and others. This powerful meditation technique involves directing loving-kindness and well-wishes towards different individuals or groups, helping to deepen one's capacity for love, kindness, and understanding.

The practice of loving-kindness meditation typically involves four distinct stages. In the first stage, practitioners focus on sending love and positive intentions towards themselves. This stage is vital as it allows individuals to develop self-compassion and learn to love and accept themselves fully. By acknowledging one's own needs for love and care, the practice builds a solid foundation for cultivating love towards others.

The second stage of loving-kindness meditation involves directing loving-kindness towards loved ones, such as family members, close friends, or partners. By focusing on those we feel close to, we deepen our understanding of what it means to care for others and develop empathy towards their joys and sorrows.

The third stage involves sending well-wishes and thoughts of loving-kindness towards neutral individuals or strangers. These can be people we encounter in our daily lives but do not have a strong emotional connection to. This stage helps to expand our capacity for compassion beyond our immediate circle, fostering a sense of interconnectedness with others.

The final stage of loving-kindness meditation focuses on difficult individuals or people we may have conflicts with. This can be particularly challenging but is a crucial step in expanding our capacity for love and understanding. By sending well-wishes and love towards those who are difficult, we cultivate empathy and learn to let go of resentment or negative emotions.

There are various guided loving-kindness meditation scripts and variations that cater to different purposes and intentions. These scripts often provide step-by-step instructions on how to cultivate loving-kindness and may incorporate visualization exercises, affirmations, or breathing techniques.

Some variations of loving-kindness meditation focus on specific areas of life, such as healing relationships, self-compassion, or cultivating forgiveness. These variations allow individuals to tailor the practice to their specific needs and intentions, providing a more personalized and meaningful experience.

It's important to remember that loving-kindness meditation is a practice that requires patience and consistency. Regularly engaging in this practice can have profound effects on our emotional well-being, helping us to develop a deeper sense of love, compassion, and empathy towards ourselves and others.

Body Scan Meditation

Meditation is a powerful practice that can help you cultivate a greater sense of self-awareness and relaxation. One form of meditation that has gained popularity in recent years is body scan meditation. This technique involves systematically scanning the body, bringing attention and awareness to different body parts. By doing so, body scan meditation can promote physical and emotional well-being.

During a body scan meditation, you start by finding a comfortable position, either sitting or lying down. Close your eyes and begin to bring your attention to your breath. Take a few deep breaths, allowing your body to relax with each exhale. Once you feel centered and present, you can begin the scanning process.

Start with your toes, bringing your attention to each individual toe and noticing any sensations or tension present. Slowly move your attention up to your feet, ankles, and calves, continuing to observe any sensations you feel. As you progress, scan through your knees, thighs, hips, and pelvis.

Continue moving your attention up through your abdomen, chest, and back, noticing any areas of tension or tightness. Bring your awareness to your shoulders, arms, and hands, taking note of any sensations you feel. Finally, scan through your neck, jaw, and face, releasing any tension you may be holding in those areas.

Throughout the body scan, it's important to approach each body part with curiosity and non-judgment. If you notice any areas of tension or discomfort, simply observe them without trying to change or fix them. By bringing awareness to these areas, you can begin to cultivate a deeper sense of body awareness and relaxation.

In addition to the traditional body scan, there are variations of this practice that you can explore. Some people find it helpful to focus on specific areas of the body that need extra attention, such as areas that are experiencing pain or discomfort. Others may choose to incorporate visualization or breathing techniques into their body scan meditation.

Body scan meditation can have numerous benefits for both your physical and emotional well-being. It can help reduce stress and anxiety, promote relaxation, and improve your overall body awareness. By regularly practicing body scan meditation, you can develop a greater sense of connection with your body and cultivate a greater sense of peace and well-being.

Understanding Chakras

Link Between Chakras and Spiritual Energy

Chakras are an important concept in the realm of spirituality, representing the flow of spiritual energy throughout the body. Understanding the link between chakras and spiritual energy is crucial for those on a spiritual journey. In this subchapter, we will delve deeper into this connection and explore how chakras play a role in spiritual energy.

The concept of chakras originated from ancient Indian traditions and has gained widespread recognition in the spiritual community. Chakras are believed to be energy centers in the body, representing different aspects of our being. They are often depicted as spinning wheels or vortexes that allow energy to flow through them.

When our chakras are balanced and aligned, the energy flows smoothly, leading to a sense of well-being, vitality, and spiritual growth. On the other hand, when our chakras are blocked or out of balance, it can result in physical, emotional, and spiritual imbalances.

The seven main chakras are typically associated with different qualities, colors, and locations in the body. Each chakra corresponds to specific aspects of our physical, emotional, and spiritual well-being. Let's explore them in more detail.

Root Chakra: Located at the base of the spine, the root chakra is associated with stability, security, and our connection to the physical world. It is represented by the color red.

Sacral Chakra: Situated in the lower abdomen, the sacral chakra is associated with creativity, passion, and our emotional well-being. It is represented by the color orange.

Solar Plexus Chakra: Found in the upper abdomen, the solar plexus chakra is linked to personal power, confidence, and self-esteem. It is represented by the color yellow.

Heart Chakra: Located in the center of the chest, the heart chakra represents love, compassion, and emotional healing. It is represented by the color green.

Throat Chakra: Situated in the throat area, the throat chakra is associated with communication, self-expression, and authenticity. It is represented by the color blue.

Third Eye Chakra: Found in the center of the forehead, between the eyebrows, the third eye chakra is connected to intuition, inner wisdom, and spiritual insight. It is represented by the color indigo.

Crown Chakra: Located at the top of the head, the crown chakra represents spiritual connection, higher consciousness, and divine wisdom. It is represented by the color violet or white.

Now that we have explored the seven main chakras and their associated qualities, colors, and locations, it is important to understand the connection between chakras, emotions, and overall well-being. Our chakras interact with our emotional state and affect our mental, physical, and spiritual health.

When our chakras are in balance, we experience emotional harmony, mental clarity, and a sense of spiritual connection. However, when there is an imbalance or blockage in any of our chakras, it can manifest as physical symptoms or emotional disturbances.

Understanding and working with our chakras can help us identify imbalances and address them through various practices such as meditation, energy healing, yoga, and other holistic approaches. By doing so, we can restore the flow of spiritual energy and promote overall well-being.

Balancing and Aligning the Chakras

Welcome to the subchapter on Balancing and Aligning the Chakras. In this section, we will discuss various techniques and practices that can help you achieve balance and alignment within your chakras. By understanding and working with the energy centers in your body, you can promote overall well-being and spiritual growth.

Chakras are subtle energy centers located within our bodies, and when they are in balance and alignment, we experience a sense of harmony and vitality. However, when our chakras are blocked or imbalanced, it can manifest as physical, emotional, or spiritual ailments. Here, we will explore some effective techniques to help you restore balance and alignment to your chakras.

One common method for balancing and aligning the chakras is through the use of meditation. By practicing specific chakra meditation techniques, you can focus your awareness on each individual chakra, allowing it to open and flow freely. Visualizations and affirmations can also be incorporated into your meditation practice to enhance the healing process.

In addition to meditation, there are various other practices that can aid in balancing and aligning the chakras. One such practice is the use of yoga postures specifically designed to target each chakra. Each yoga pose is associated with a particular chakra, and by practicing these poses, you can activate and harmonize the energy within each chakra.

Another effective technique for balancing the chakras is through the use of breathwork or pranayama. By consciously controlling your breath and directing it to specific energy centers, you can remove blockages and restore the natural flow of energy. Deep, slow breathing exercises and alternate nostril breathing are particularly beneficial for chakra balancing.

Sound therapy is another modality that can be used to bring balance and alignment to the chakras. Each chakra is associated with a specific sound or frequency, and by listening to or chanting these sounds, you can stimulate and harmonize the energy centers. Singing bowls, tuning forks, and mantras are commonly used in sound therapy for chakra healing.

Crystal healing is another practice that can assist in balancing and aligning the chakras. Each chakra is associated with a particular crystal or gemstone, and by placing these stones on or near the corresponding energy centers, you can help clear blockages and restore energy flow. Crystals such as amethyst, lapis lazuli, and citrine are often used in chakra healing.

Reiki, a form of energy healing, is also effective in balancing and aligning the chakras. By channeling universal life force energy, a Reiki practitioner can remove blockages and replenish the energy within each chakra. Receiving a Reiki session can promote deep relaxation and energetic healing.

By incorporating these techniques and practices into your daily routine, you can promote balance and alignment within your chakras, leading to improved overall well-being and spiritual growth. Remember to listen to your body and intuition when working with your chakras, as everyone's journey is unique. With dedication and practice, you can achieve optimal health and harmony within your energy centers.

Chakra Meditation Practices

Meditation is a powerful practice for activating and harmonizing our chakras, the energy centers in our body. By focusing our attention on specific techniques, we can increase energy flow and achieve spiritual awakening. In this subchapter, we will explore various chakra meditation practices that can help you enhance your chakra awareness and experience transformation.

Each chakra corresponds to different aspects of our physical, mental, and spiritual well-being. By understanding and working with these energy centers, we can cultivate balance and harmony within ourselves. Let's dive into specific meditation techniques for each chakra:

The Root Chakra Meditation: The root chakra is associated with our sense of grounding and stability. To activate and harmonize this chakra, try practicing a grounding meditation. Find a quiet and comfortable space to sit. Close your eyes and take a few deep breaths. Visualize a stream of red energy flowing from the base of your spine down into the earth, anchoring you to the ground. As you inhale, imagine this energy flowing up through your body, nourishing and strengthening your root chakra.

The Sacral Chakra Meditation: The sacral chakra relates to our creativity, passion, and sensuality. To awaken this chakra, you can practice a sacral chakra meditation. Sit in a comfortable position and close your eyes. Take a few deep breaths and focus your attention on your lower abdomen, where the sacral chakra is located. Visualize an orange light glowing in this area, becoming brighter with each inhale. As you exhale, release any blocked energy or emotions associated with this chakra.

The Solar Plexus Chakra Meditation: The solar plexus chakra is connected to our personal power and self-esteem. To activate and balance this chakra, try a solar plexus chakra meditation. Sit comfortably and take a few deep breaths. Imagine a golden sun radiating warmth and energy in your stomach area, where the solar plexus chakra resides. With each inhale, feel this sun expanding and empowering you. As you exhale, release any self-doubt or insecurity that may be blocking this chakra.

The Heart Chakra Meditation: The heart chakra governs our ability to give and receive love. To open and align this chakra, practice a heart chakra meditation. Find a quiet and peaceful space to sit. Close your eyes and take a few deep breaths. Visualize a green light glowing in the center of your chest, at the level of your heart. As you breathe in and out, imagine this light expanding and enveloping your entire body, filling you with love and compassion.

The Throat Chakra Meditation: The throat chakra is associated with clear communication and self-expression. To activate this chakra, try a throat chakra meditation. Sit comfortably and close your eyes. Take a few deep breaths and focus your attention on your throat area. Visualize a beautiful blue light spinning and expanding in this region with each inhale. As you exhale, release any tension or fear that may be blocking your ability to express yourself authentically.

The Third Eye Chakra Meditation: The third eye chakra is connected to intuition and spiritual insight. To awaken this chakra, practice a third eye chakra meditation. Find a quiet and stable position to sit. Close your eyes and take a few deep breaths. Direct your attention to the space between your eyebrows, where the third eye chakra is located. Visualize an indigo light glowing and pulsating in this area, enhancing your inner vision and wisdom.

The Crown Chakra Meditation: The crown chakra represents our connection to the divine and spiritual enlightenment. To activate and harmonize this chakra, try a crown chakra meditation. Sit comfortably and close your eyes. Take a few deep breaths and visualize a brilliant white light above your head, symbolizing the crown chakra. As you inhale, imagine this light entering through the top of your head and cascading down your body, infusing you with divine wisdom and cosmic energy.

Chakra meditation offers numerous benefits, including increased energy flow and spiritual awakening. By practicing regular chakra meditations, you can enhance your overall well-being and experience a deeper connection with your spiritual self. Let's explore some of the key benefits of chakra meditation:

- **Increased Energy Flow:** Chakra meditation helps to remove any blockages or imbalances in the energy centers, allowing for a smooth and balanced flow of energy throughout the body. This can result in increased vitality and a greater sense of well-being.
- **Spiritual Awakening:** By working with the chakras, we can awaken our spiritual potential and deepen our connection with the divine. Chakra meditation can help us access higher states of consciousness, gain spiritual insights, and experience a sense of oneness with the universe.
- **Balanced Emotions:** Chakra meditation can aid in releasing and balancing emotions that may be stored in our energy centers. By bringing awareness to our chakras and using specific meditation techniques, we can navigate through emotional blockages and achieve emotional harmony.
- **Enhanced Intuition:** Chakra meditation can open our third eye chakra, the center of intuition and inner wisdom. With regular practice, we can cultivate and trust our intuitive abilities, making better decisions and gaining a deeper understanding of ourselves and the world around us.

Now that you have explored the specific techniques and benefits of chakra meditation, it's time to put them into practice. The following guided chakra meditation scripts and visualizations will help you enhance your chakra awareness and facilitate transformation:

- **Root Chakra Meditation:** Visualize a red energy flowing from the base of your spine down into the earth, grounding and connecting you to the earth's energy.
- **Sacral Chakra Meditation:** Imagine an orange light glowing in your lower abdomen, radiating warmth and creativity.
- **Solar Plexus Chakra Meditation:** Visualize a golden sun in your stomach area, empowering and strengthening your sense of personal power and self-esteem.
- **Heart Chakra Meditation:** Picture a green light expanding from the center of your chest, filling you with love, compassion, and interconnectedness.
- **Throat Chakra Meditation:** Visualize a blue light spinning and expanding in your throat area, allowing you to express yourself authentically and communicate with clarity.

- **Third Eye Chakra Meditation:** Imagine an indigo light pulsating in the space between your eyebrows, opening your inner vision and connecting you to spiritual insights.
- **Crown Chakra Meditation:** Visualize a brilliant white light above your head, symbolizing your connection to the divine and the infinite wisdom of the universe.

By incorporating these guided chakra meditations into your daily practice, you can experience deep transformation and align your energy centers for optimal well-being.

Mindfulness for Stress Reduction

Mindfulness-Based Stress Reduction (MBSR)

Mindfulness-Based Stress Reduction (MBSR) is a powerful tool for managing stress and enhancing overall well-being. It combines the ancient practice of mindfulness meditation with modern psychology to help individuals cultivate a greater sense of calm, clarity, and resilience in the face of life's challenges.

MBSR was developed by Dr. Jon Kabat-Zinn in the late 1970s at the University of Massachusetts Medical School. He recognized the need for a structured program that could help individuals cope with stress, pain, and illness in a holistic way. Since its inception, MBSR has gained widespread recognition and has been implemented in various settings, including hospitals, clinics, corporate offices, and schools.

One of the core principles of MBSR is the cultivation of mindfulness. Mindfulness is the practice of paying attention to the present moment with curiosity and non-judgment. It involves gently bringing the mind back to the present whenever it wanders, without getting caught up in thoughts, emotions, or judgments.

Through mindfulness meditation, individuals learn to observe their thoughts and emotions without getting carried away by them. This allows them to develop a greater sense of self-awareness and to notice patterns of stress and reactivity in their lives. With this awareness, they can then choose to respond to stressors in a more skillful and compassionate way.

Another key component of MBSR is body awareness. The body is a valuable source of information and can serve as an anchor to the present moment. MBSR teaches individuals to pay attention to sensations in the body, such as the breath, physical tension, or sensations of warmth or coolness.

By bringing attention to the body, individuals can develop a greater sense of embodiment and connectedness. They can also learn to recognize physical signs of stress and tension, and respond to them with relaxation techniques such as deep breathing or progressive muscle relaxation.

Research studies have shown that MBSR can have significant benefits for those who practice it regularly. It has been found to reduce symptoms of anxiety, depression, and chronic pain, as well as improve sleep quality and enhance overall well-being. MBSR has also been shown to increase resilience and improve the ability to cope with stress.

Furthermore, neuroimaging studies have revealed that MBSR can actually change the structure and function of the brain. It has been found to increase activity in areas of the brain associated with attention, emotion regulation, and perspective-taking. These changes in the brain can lead to lasting improvements in mental and emotional well-being.

In conclusion, Mindfulness-Based Stress Reduction (MBSR) is an effective and evidence-based approach to stress management. By cultivating mindfulness and body awareness, individuals can develop a greater sense of calm, clarity, and resilience in their lives. The research supports the effectiveness of MBSR in reducing stress and enhancing overall well-being, making it a valuable tool for individuals seeking to manage the stresses of everyday life.

Mindfulness Techniques for Anxiety

When it comes to managing anxiety and panic attacks, mindfulness techniques can be extremely beneficial. By practicing mindfulness, you can learn to cultivate present-moment awareness and reduce anxiety symptoms. In this subchapter, we will explore various mindfulness techniques specifically designed for addressing anxiety and promoting relaxation.

Mindfulness involves being fully present in the current moment, without judgment. It can help you become more aware of your thoughts, emotions, and physical sensations, allowing you to gain a greater sense of control over anxiety. Here are some mindfulness techniques that can be effective in managing anxiety:

1. Deep Breathing: Take slow, deep breaths, focusing your attention on the sensation of your breath entering and leaving your body. This practice can help calm your nervous system and reduce anxiety.
2. Body Scan: Start from the top of your head and gradually move your attention down through your body, paying close attention to each area. Notice any sensations or tension you may be holding and allow them to release.
3. Thought Labeling: When anxiety-causing thoughts arise, observe them without judgment and label them as thoughts. This practice can help you detach from your thoughts and reduce their power over you.
4. Sensory Awareness: Engage your senses by focusing on the present moment. Notice the tastes, smells, sounds, sights, and textures around you. This can help shift your attention away from anxious thoughts.
5. Progressive Muscle Relaxation: Tense and relax each muscle group in your body, starting from your toes and working your way up to your head. This technique can help release tension and promote relaxation.
6. Guided Imagery: Visualize a calm and peaceful place in your mind, such as a beach or a forest. Engage your senses and imagine yourself in that environment, allowing yourself to experience a sense of relaxation.

By incorporating these mindfulness techniques into your daily routine, you can develop a greater sense of calm and manage anxiety more effectively. Practice each technique regularly to build your mindfulness skills and reduce anxiety symptoms.

Coping with Stress through Meditation

Exploring various meditation techniques and practices for coping with stress and promoting relaxation:

Meditation is a powerful tool for managing stress and promoting a state of relaxation. There are numerous meditation techniques that can be used to achieve these benefits. One popular technique is mindfulness meditation, which involves focusing your attention on the present moment and accepting it without judgment. By cultivating mindfulness, you can reduce stress and improve your overall well-being.

Another effective technique is guided imagery, where you visualize peaceful and calming scenes to help relax your mind and body. This practice can transport you to a serene location and induce a deep sense of relaxation.

Breathing exercises are also commonly used in meditation to reduce stress. By taking slow, deep breaths and focusing on your breath, you can activate your body's relaxation response and calm your mind.

Body scan meditation involves systematically scanning your body for any tension or discomfort and releasing it through deep breathing and relaxation techniques. This practice helps you develop body awareness and promotes deep relaxation.

These are just a few examples of the many meditation techniques available to help you cope with stress and promote relaxation. It's important to find the technique that resonates with you and incorporate it into your daily routine.

Discussing the benefits of meditation in reducing stress hormones and calming the nervous system:

Meditation has been scientifically proven to reduce stress hormones like cortisol and adrenaline. When we are stressed, these hormones flood our system and can lead to a wide range of physical and mental health problems. By practicing meditation regularly, we can counteract the effects of stress by activating the body's relaxation response and lowering the levels of stress hormones in the body. This has a calming effect on the nervous system and helps restore balance and harmony.

Moreover, meditation has been shown to increase the production of feel-good hormones like serotonin and dopamine, which can elevate mood and reduce anxiety and depression. It also improves the quality of sleep and enhances overall well-being.

Additionally, meditation enhances brain function and increases focus, concentration, and clarity of thought. This can be particularly beneficial for those who struggle with racing thoughts and a busy mind. By training the mind to be present and focused through meditation, we can better manage stress and improve cognitive abilities.

Guided stress-reducing meditations and visualizations for relieving stress and promoting calmness:

To help you relieve stress and promote calmness, here are a few guided meditations and visualizations:

1. Progressive Muscle Relaxation: This guided meditation involves tensing and releasing each muscle group in your body, helping you achieve deep physical and mental relaxation.

2. Nature Visualization: Close your eyes and imagine yourself in a peaceful natural setting, such as a tranquil beach or a serene forest. Engage all your senses to fully immerse yourself in the calming experience.

3. Loving-Kindness Meditation: Focus on sending love, kindness, and well-wishes to yourself and others. This meditation cultivates compassion, gratitude, and a sense of interconnectedness.

4. Breath Awareness: Pay attention to your breath and let go of any thoughts or distractions. This simple practice helps calm the mind and brings you back to the present moment.

Remember, the key to effective guided meditations and visualizations is to find ones that resonate with you and make you feel calm and relaxed. Experiment with different techniques and explore what works best for you.

Spiritual Evolution and Growth

Spiritual Awakening and Awareness

Throughout history, spiritual awakening has been a profound catalyst for transformation, leading individuals to expand their consciousness and enhance their perception of the world around them. This process involves a deepening connection to one's inner self, the universe, and the divine. In this subchapter, we will explore the concept of spiritual awakening and its powerful effects on awareness.

Spiritual awakening is a profound shift in consciousness that brings about a heightened sense of awareness and a deep connection to the spiritual realm. It is often accompanied by a sense of clarity, inner peace, and the recognition of a greater purpose in life.

Signs of spiritual awakening can vary from person to person, but some common experiences include a sudden desire for self-discovery, increased intuition, a greater sense of empathy towards others, and an enhanced connection to nature. You may also start to question the meaning of life, your beliefs, and societal norms.

There are several stages to the process of spiritual awakening. Initially, one may experience a period of dissatisfaction or a feeling of being lost. This can be followed by intense emotional and psychological healing, as well as a deepening connection to spirituality. Eventually, there is a sense of integration, where the awakened individual begins to live in alignment with their higher self and experiences a profound sense of purpose and fulfillment.

Integrating spiritual experiences is an important aspect of the awakening process. It involves incorporating these profound experiences into daily life and finding ways to maintain a balanced and grounded state of being. This can be achieved through various practices such as meditation, journaling, yoga, and spending time in nature.

Cultivating spiritual awareness is key to supporting ongoing growth and development. It involves tuning in to your inner self, listening to your intuition, and being open to the messages and guidance of the universe. This can be achieved through practices such as mindfulness, self-reflection, and engaging in spiritual rituals and ceremonies.

In conclusion, spiritual awakening and awareness have the power to profoundly transform our consciousness and perception of the world. By exploring the signs and stages of awakening and integrating spiritual experiences into our daily lives, we can cultivate a deeper connection to our higher selves and the spiritual realm.

Spiritual Transformation and Self-Realization

The path of spiritual transformation and self-realization is a profound journey that opens doors to a greater understanding of ourselves, the world around us, and our connection to a higher power. It is a process through which we seek to transcend our limitations, evolve our consciousness, and find our true purpose in life.

During this journey, we embark on a quest of self-discovery and self-acceptance, peeling away the layers of conditioning and societal expectations to uncover our authentic selves. We learn to let go of the ego, the false sense of identity that often holds us back from experiencing the fullness of our being.

At the heart of spiritual transformation is the dissolution of the ego - the identification with our thoughts, emotions, and external circumstances. As we release our attachment to these transient aspects of our existence, we can begin to awaken to higher levels of consciousness and tap into the universal source of wisdom and love.

Through various practices and teachings, we can cultivate self-awareness, presence, and mindfulness. These practices may include meditation, breathwork, yoga, journaling, and contemplative inquiry, among others. They help us quiet the mind, still our restless thoughts, and connect with our innermost essence.

As we engage in these practices, we develop a deeper sense of self-acceptance and compassion, embracing all parts of ourselves with love and understanding. We learn to let go of judgment and self-criticism, recognizing that we are all inherently divine and deserving of love and acceptance.

Spiritual enlightenment is not an endpoint but rather an ongoing process. It is a continuous journey of growth, learning, and self-transformation. It invites us to embody our spiritual insights and integrate them into our daily lives.

In conclusion, the path of spiritual transformation and self-realization is a profound and transformative journey that requires dedication, commitment, and an open heart. Through practices and teachings aimed at self-discovery, self-acceptance, and spiritual enlightenment, we can unlock our true potential and experience a deep sense of fulfillment and inner peace.

The Path to Spiritual Enlightenment

The path to spiritual enlightenment is a journey that many individuals embark on in order to seek a greater understanding of themselves and the universe. It is a deeply personal and transformative process, often guided by spiritual traditions and practices. In this subchapter, we will explore different paths and practices that can lead to spiritual enlightenment.

Throughout history, various spiritual paths and traditions have emerged, each offering a unique approach to achieving spiritual enlightenment. These paths can include religious traditions, such as Buddhism, Hinduism, or Christianity, as well as non-religious practices, such as mindfulness and self-inquiry.

One of the first steps in embarking on the path to spiritual enlightenment is exploring different spiritual paths and traditions. This can involve reading books, attending lectures, and engaging in discussions with practitioners of various traditions. By gaining exposure to different perspectives, you can broaden your understanding and choose a path that resonates with your beliefs and values.

Once you have chosen a spiritual path, it is important to engage in regular spiritual practices. These practices serve as a means of deepening your connection with the divine and cultivating a state of spiritual awareness. Meditation is a powerful practice that can quiet the mind and open the door to higher states of consciousness. By setting aside dedicated time for meditation, you can cultivate a sense of peace and clarity.

Mindfulness is another essential practice on the path to spiritual enlightenment. It involves being fully present in the moment and cultivating an attitude of non-judgmental awareness. By practicing mindfulness in everyday life, you can cultivate greater self-awareness and deepen your connection with the present moment.

Self-inquiry is another powerful tool for spiritual awakening. It involves questioning the nature of our existence and seeking to understand the true nature of our selves. Through deep introspection and self-reflection, we can shed limiting beliefs and discover our true essence.

One of the key principles on the path to spiritual enlightenment is surrender and letting go. This involves surrendering our attachment to outcomes and releasing control. By surrendering to the flow of life and trusting in the divine, we can open ourselves up to higher states of consciousness and spiritual awakening.

In conclusion, the path to spiritual enlightenment is a deeply personal journey that can be pursued through various spiritual paths and practices. By exploring different traditions, engaging in spiritual practices such as meditation and mindfulness, and cultivating a mindset of surrender, we can embark on a transformative journey of spiritual awakening and enlightenment.

The Power of Manifestation

Utilizing Mindfulness in Manifestation

When it comes to manifestation and creating positive life changes, mindfulness can play a crucial role. Mindfulness is the practice of being fully present and aware of our thoughts, emotions, and actions. By cultivating mindfulness, we can align ourselves with our desires and manifest them into reality. In this subchapter, we will explore how to utilize mindfulness in the manifestation process.

One technique for utilizing mindfulness in manifestation is to start by setting clear intentions. This involves clarifying what we truly desire and setting specific goals for ourselves. By being mindful of our intentions, we can focus our thoughts and energy towards achieving them.

In addition to setting intentions, it's important to cultivate a positive mindset. Mindfulness can help us become aware of any negative or limiting beliefs that may be holding us back. By acknowledging these beliefs and replacing them with positive affirmations, we can align our thoughts with our desires.

Another way to use mindfulness in manifestation is by staying present in the moment. Oftentimes, we can get caught up in worrying about the future or dwelling on the past. By practicing mindfulness and staying present, we can avoid getting caught in negative thought patterns and instead focus on the present moment, where manifestation happens.

Furthermore, mindfulness can help us become aware of any resistance or blocks that may be hindering our manifestation process. By observing our thoughts and emotions without judgment, we can identify any areas of resistance and work through them. This may involve releasing old beliefs, practicing self-compassion, or seeking support from others.

Lastly, mindfulness can be integrated into our daily activities and rituals. By bringing mindfulness to everyday tasks such as eating, exercising, or even brushing our teeth, we can cultivate a sense of presence and gratitude. This helps us stay aligned with our desires and create positive changes in our lives.

In conclusion, utilizing mindfulness in the manifestation process is a powerful tool for creating positive life changes. By setting clear intentions, cultivating a positive mindset, staying present, addressing resistance, and integrating mindfulness into daily activities, we can align our thoughts, emotions, and actions with our desired outcomes. So, let's embrace mindfulness and watch as our dreams become a reality.

Law of Attraction and Mindfulness

The Law of Attraction and mindfulness are two powerful principles that can work in harmony to shape our reality and manifest our desires. In this subchapter, we will explore the relationship between these two concepts and how mindfulness enhances the effectiveness of the Law of Attraction.

The Law of Attraction is the belief that like attracts like, and that our thoughts and beliefs shape our reality. It teaches us that by focusing on positive thoughts and beliefs, we can attract positive experiences and outcomes into our lives. Mindfulness, on the other hand, involves the practice of being fully present in the moment and non-judgmentally aware of our thoughts and feelings.

By incorporating mindfulness into our practice of the Law of Attraction, we can heighten our awareness of our thoughts and ensure that they align with our desired manifestations. When we are mindful, we are better able to recognize negative or limiting beliefs that may be blocking our desires from manifesting. We can then consciously choose to replace these beliefs with positive and empowering ones.

One of the key benefits of mindfulness in relation to the Law of Attraction is that it helps us to cultivate a positive mindset. When we are mindful, we are more likely to focus on the present moment and appreciate the abundance and blessings that already exist in our lives. This positive mindset acts as a magnet for attracting more positive experiences and manifestations.

In addition to cultivating a positive mindset, mindfulness also helps to increase our emotional intelligence and resilience. It allows us to observe our thoughts and emotions without getting caught up in them or reacting impulsively. By developing this level of awareness, we can respond to challenges and setbacks with greater clarity and composure, without allowing negativity to derail us from our manifestation journey.

To harness the Law of Attraction effectively, it is essential to integrate mindfulness practices into our daily routine. This can include engaging in mindful meditation, journaling, or visualization exercises. These practices help us to quiet our minds, focus our intention, and align our thoughts and beliefs with our desired manifestations.

In the next section, we will delve deeper into the importance of cultivating a positive mindset and aligning with our desired manifestations. We will explore practical strategies and techniques for shifting our mindset and overcoming any limiting beliefs that may be holding us back from manifesting our desires.

Visualization and Affirmation Practices

The practice of visualization and affirmation is a powerful tool for manifesting our desired outcomes. By consciously creating vivid mental images and using positive statements, we can align our thoughts, beliefs, and emotions with what we want to attract into our lives. In this subchapter, we will explore some effective visualization and affirmation practices that can help you tap into the law of attraction and manifest your dreams.

Visualization is the process of creating detailed mental images of the outcomes we desire. It involves using our imagination to see, feel, and experience our goals as if they have already become a reality. When we visualize, we activate the same neural pathways in our brain as when we actually experience something in reality. This helps to program our subconscious mind and increases the likelihood of manifesting our desires.

Affirmations, on the other hand, are positive statements that we repeat to ourselves with the intention of shifting our beliefs and mindset. By affirming what we want as if it has already happened, we send a powerful message to our subconscious mind that helps to eliminate any doubts or limiting beliefs that may be holding us back.

To begin your visualization and affirmation practice, find a quiet and comfortable space where you can relax and focus. Close your eyes and take a few deep breaths to center yourself. Now, imagine yourself in the specific situation or outcome you desire. See the details of this vision clearly in your mind's eye - the colors, the sounds, the smells, and the emotions associated with it.

As you hold this vision, start repeating your affirmations. Choose affirmations that resonate with you and evoke a sense of belief and excitement. For example, if you want to attract financial abundance, your affirmation could be I am a magnet for money and prosperity. I easily attract opportunities to create wealth. Repeat these affirmations with conviction and visualize yourself living the abundant life you desire.

It's important to remember that visualization and affirmation practices work best when accompanied by strong emotions. Feel the joy, gratitude, and excitement as if your desires have already been fulfilled. The more you can evoke these positive emotions, the more powerful your practice will be in attracting your desired outcomes.

Remember to practice your visualization and affirmation exercises regularly. Set aside dedicated time each day to immerse yourself in the practice. Over time, you will notice a shift in your beliefs, mindset, and actions, which will align with your desires and help you manifest them into reality.

Healing through Mindfulness and Meditation

Mind-Body Connection in Healing

The mind-body connection plays a vital role in the healing process. Our thoughts, emotions, and beliefs have a profound impact on our physical health and overall well-being. Understanding and harnessing this connection can be a powerful tool for spiritual growth and healing.

When it comes to healing, it is important to recognize that our bodies and minds are interconnected. The way we think and feel can directly influence our physical health. Research has shown that stress and negative emotions can weaken the immune system, making us more susceptible to illness and disease.

By exploring and understanding the mind-body connection, we can learn to actively participate in our own healing process. We can tap into the power of our thoughts and beliefs to promote overall wellness and recovery.

Mindfulness and meditation are two practices that can greatly enhance the mind-body connection and support healing. Mindfulness involves being fully present in the moment, paying attention to our thoughts, feelings, and bodily sensations without judgment. This practice allows us to become more aware of the mind-body connection and cultivate a greater sense of well-being.

Meditation is a powerful tool for relaxing the body and quieting the mind. By taking a few moments each day to sit in meditation, we can reduce stress, lower blood pressure, and promote a state of deep relaxation. This can have a profound impact on our physical health, as well as our emotional and spiritual well-being.

Through mindfulness and meditation, we can learn to cultivate a deeper sense of self-awareness and self-compassion. We can develop the ability to respond to stress and negative emotions in a healthier and more constructive way. By incorporating these practices into our daily lives, we can support our overall healing process and enhance our spiritual growth.

Mindfulness for Pain Management

In today's fast-paced world, many individuals are seeking alternative methods for managing acute and chronic pain. One approach that has gained significant attention is the practice of mindfulness. Mindfulness involves being fully present in the moment, paying attention to our thoughts and feelings without judgment. It can be a powerful tool for pain management, allowing individuals to develop a new relationship with their pain and ultimately find relief.

Throughout this subchapter, we will explore the role of mindfulness in managing pain and discuss various techniques that can be used to cultivate non-judgmental awareness and acceptance of pain. Additionally, we will delve into the world of guided mindfulness meditations and visualizations, offering practical exercises that can be used to alleviate pain and enhance overall quality of life.

Mindfulness for pain management begins with acknowledging the mind-body connection. Research has shown that our thoughts, emotions, and beliefs can influence our perception of pain. By increasing our awareness of these mental and emotional factors, we can begin to shift our relationship with pain and develop a more compassionate and accepting stance.

One technique that can be particularly helpful in cultivating non-judgmental awareness and acceptance of pain is the body scan. This practice involves systematically bringing our attention to different parts of the body, noticing any sensations or discomfort without judgment. By developing a curious and open attitude towards our pain, we can learn to observe it without becoming overwhelmed or consumed by it.

In addition to the body scan, mindfulness meditation can be a powerful tool for managing pain. During meditation, we can focus our attention on the present moment, using techniques such as breath awareness or loving-kindness meditation. This can help to shift our focus away from the pain and towards a state of calm and relaxation. Regular practice of mindfulness meditation has been shown to reduce pain intensity and improve overall well-being.

Furthermore, visualizations can be a valuable component of a mindfulness practice for pain relief. Through visualization, we can imagine ourselves in a peaceful and soothing environment, engaging all of our senses to create a vivid mental image. This can provide a temporary escape from the pain and promote a sense of comfort and relaxation.

Overall, the practice of mindfulness offers individuals a unique and empowering approach to managing acute and chronic pain. By cultivating non-judgmental awareness and acceptance of pain through techniques such as the body scan, mindfulness meditation, and visualizations, individuals can start to develop a new relationship with their pain and find relief. Through the implementation of these mindfulness practices, individuals can tap into their inner strength and enhance their overall quality of life.

Meditative Practices for Emotional Healing

Emotional healing is a deeply personal journey that requires gentle introspection and a willingness to let go of past traumas and emotional wounds. In this subchapter, we will explore various meditative practices that can aid in the process of emotional healing and offer you a path towards resilience and inner peace.

Meditation has been used for centuries as a tool for healing, and it holds great power in helping us process and release emotional baggage. Through mindfulness and focused awareness, we can begin to uncover the roots of our emotional pain and start the process of letting go.

One powerful meditative practice for emotional healing is breathwork meditation. Deep, intentional breathing allows us to connect with our body and release stuck emotions. By focusing on our breath and allowing it to flow in and out naturally, we create a calming rhythm that helps us access deeper layers of our emotional being.

Another effective technique is body scan meditation. By systematically bringing our attention to different parts of our body and observing any sensations or tensions that arise, we can identify and release emotional blockages. This practice helps us develop a greater sense of body awareness and allows us to connect with and process emotions that may be stored in different areas of our body.

Visualizations and guided imagery are also powerful tools for emotional healing. By creating vivid mental images and engaging our senses, we can tap into the healing power of our imagination. Guided meditations that lead us through visualizations of peaceful landscapes, healing light, or compassionate beings can help us release negative emotions and cultivate feelings of love, forgiveness, and acceptance.

Self-compassion and self-forgiveness are essential components of emotional healing. It is crucial to approach ourselves with kindness and understanding as we navigate through our emotional wounds. Through meditation, we can cultivate self-compassion by directing loving-kindness towards ourselves. This practice involves repeating affirmations such as May I be happy, may I be healthy, may I be at peace and extending those wishes to others as well.

As you embark on your journey of emotional healing, it is important to remember that patience and self-care are key. Allow yourself the time and space to fully immerse in these meditative practices and be gentle with yourself along the way. Through consistent practice and an open heart, you will begin to experience a profound transformation and discover the inner peace that resides within you.

Enhancing Intuition and Inner Wisdom

Developing Intuition through Meditation

In today's fast-paced world, many individuals are seeking ways to connect with their inner selves and tap into their intuition. Meditation has long been recognized as a powerful tool for self-discovery and personal growth. It offers a pathway to delving deeper into our consciousness, allowing us to access our intuitive wisdom and make better decisions in life.

Meditation acts as a gateway to developing and honing our intuition. It helps us to quiet the mind, create space for inner reflection, and cultivate a heightened sense of awareness. Through the practice of meditation, we can explore the connection between our meditative state and the development of our intuition.

One technique that is particularly effective for developing intuition through meditation is mindfulness. Mindfulness involves being fully present and non-judgmentally aware of our thoughts, emotions, and sensations in the present moment. By practicing mindfulness during meditation, we can learn to recognize the subtle messages from our intuition.

Another technique for developing intuition through meditation is visualizations. This involves using the power of our imagination to create vivid mental images that allow us to tap into our intuitive wisdom. By visualizing a specific situation or question, we can access insights and guidance that may not be readily apparent in our everyday conscious awareness.

A third technique for developing intuition through meditation is breathwork. Our breath is an anchor that can help us cultivate a deep state of relaxation and focus. By bringing our attention to the breath during meditation, we can quiet the mind and open ourselves up to receiving intuitive messages and guidance.

It is important to note that developing intuition through meditation is a process that takes time and practice. It requires us to cultivate patience, trust, and an openness to receiving insights. As we continue to explore the connection between meditation and intuition, we may find that our intuitive abilities become more refined and accessible.

In summary, meditation serves as a powerful tool for developing intuition. Through techniques such as mindfulness, visualizations, and breathwork, we can quiet the mind, tap into our intuitive wisdom, and make more informed decisions in life. With consistency and practice, we can further deepen our connection to our intuition and experience its transformative power.

Accessing Inner Guidance and Wisdom

Connecting with your inner guidance and accessing higher wisdom can be a transformative practice that brings clarity and guidance into your life. In this subchapter, we will explore various techniques and exercises to help you access your inner wisdom and make intuitive decisions.

When it comes to connecting with inner guidance, it's important to create a daily practice that allows you to quiet your mind and tap into a deeper level of awareness. This can be done through techniques such as meditation, journaling, or even spending time in nature.

Meditation is a powerful tool for accessing inner guidance. Find a quiet and comfortable place to sit, close your eyes, and focus on your breath. Allow your thoughts to float by like clouds in the sky, without attaching any judgment or significance to them. As you continue to practice this, you will find that your mind becomes more calm and clear, creating space for intuitive insights to emerge.

Journaling is another effective method for connecting with your inner guidance. Set aside a few minutes each day to write down your thoughts, feelings, and any insights that come to you. The act of putting pen to paper helps to deepen your connection with your inner wisdom and allows for greater self-reflection.

Spending time in nature can also be incredibly grounding and supportive of accessing inner wisdom. Take walks in the park, sit by a lake, or simply spend time in your backyard. As you connect with the natural world around you, you may find that your intuition becomes more heightened and your inner guidance becomes clearer.

Tuning into your intuition and receiving intuitive messages is an essential aspect of connecting with your inner guidance. There are various techniques you can practice to enhance your intuitive abilities.

One technique is learning to trust your gut feelings. Your gut often provides subtle signals about what feels right or wrong in a situation. Pay attention to these feelings and learn to trust them, even if they don't seem logical at first.

Meditation can also be useful for tuning into your intuition. During your meditation practice, set the intention to receive intuitive messages. Allow yourself to be open and receptive to any insights or guidance that may come to you.

Another technique is practicing active listening. This involves paying close attention to the subtle messages and whispers from your intuition. Slow down and observe the thoughts and ideas that come to you throughout the day. You may find that your intuition is communicating with you through these subtle clues.

Guided meditations and exercises can be powerful tools for accessing inner wisdom and making intuitive decisions. These practices can help you tap into a deeper level of awareness and receive guidance in a structured and guided manner.

One guided meditation you can try is visualizing a wise and loving presence. Close your eyes, take a few deep breaths, and imagine a wise and loving figure standing in front of you. Ask this figure any questions you have and listen for any guidance or messages that come to you.

Another exercise is called intuitive decision making. When faced with a decision, take a moment to quiet your mind and connect with your inner wisdom. Ask yourself what feels right in your body and what aligns with your higher purpose. Trust the intuitive insights that arise and use them to inform your decision-making process.

Remember, accessing your inner guidance and wisdom is a practice that takes time and patience. Be gentle with yourself as you explore these techniques and allow yourself to develop a deeper connection with your intuition.

Intuitive Practices for Decision-Making

Welcome to the subchapter on Intuitive Practices for Decision-Making. In this section, we will explore various techniques and exercises that can help you tap into your intuition and make informed decisions that are aligned with your true desires and values.

Intuition is a powerful tool that can guide us in both our personal and professional lives. It allows us to tap into our inner wisdom and make decisions that go beyond logic and reason. By embracing our intuition, we can navigate through life with more clarity, confidence, and authenticity.

One of the first steps in developing your intuitive decision-making skills is to explore the benefits that it can bring to your life. Intuitive decision-making can help you cut through the noise, trust your gut instincts, and make choices that are in alignment with your higher self. Whether you are facing a career decision or a personal dilemma, tapping into your intuition can provide you with valuable insights and guidance.

Next, let's discuss techniques for discerning intuitive insights from fears and limiting beliefs. Sometimes, our fears and beliefs can cloud our intuition and prevent us from making truly aligned decisions. By recognizing and acknowledging these fears and limiting beliefs, we can distinguish them from our true intuitive guidance. Techniques such as journaling, meditation, and self-reflection can be used to uncover and release these blocks, allowing us to access our intuition more freely.

Finally, we will dive into guided exercises for using mindfulness and intuition to make informed and aligned decisions. These exercises will help you cultivate a deeper sense of self-awareness, connect with your intuition, and gain clarity on the choices you need to make. From visualization exercises to body awareness techniques, you will have a variety of practices to choose from that resonate with you and your unique intuitive style.

Remember, the key to developing your intuitive decision-making skills is practice and trust. The more you listen to your intuition and act upon its guidance, the stronger and more reliable it will become. So, let's dive into these intuitive practices and embark on a journey of self-discovery and empowered decision-making.

Meditation for Spiritual Connection

Spiritual Awakening through Meditation

Meditation has long been known as a powerful tool for facilitating spiritual awakening and accessing higher states of consciousness. In this section, we will explore how meditation can lead to profound spiritual experiences and the expansion of one's awareness.

Through sustained meditation practice, individuals can transcend the limitations of the ego and connect with higher realms of reality. This process often involves quieting the mind, letting go of attachment to thoughts and desires, and cultivating a deep sense of presence.

There are various techniques that can aid in transcending the ego and accessing higher states of consciousness. One such technique is mindfulness meditation, which involves focusing one's attention on the present moment and observing thoughts and sensations without judgment.

Another technique is loving-kindness meditation, where individuals cultivate feelings of compassion and goodwill towards oneself, others, and the world. This practice can help dissolve the egoic boundaries and foster a sense of interconnectedness.

Furthermore, transcendental meditation, which involves chanting a specific mantra, has been found to be effective in quieting the mind and promoting spiritual experiences.

To deepen spiritual connection and experience oneness, guided meditations can be incredibly beneficial. These guided meditations provide instructions and visualizations that can assist individuals in exploring different aspects of their consciousness and connecting with their inner spiritual essence.

Practices such as breathwork, visualization, and chanting can also be incorporated to enhance the meditation experience and facilitate spiritual awakening.

By regularly engaging in meditation and exploring different practices, individuals can deepen their spiritual connection, expand their consciousness, and experience a profound sense of oneness with the universe.

Connecting with Higher Consciousness

In order to establish a deeper connection with the divine and tap into higher realms of consciousness, it is essential to explore various practices. These practices can help us unlock our spiritual potential and access a state of higher awareness. Let's delve into some effective techniques that can assist us in connecting with higher consciousness.

Spiritual communion is the process of establishing a direct and intimate connection with the divine. It involves opening our hearts and minds to receive divine guidance, wisdom, and inspiration. This communion allows us to tap into the infinite knowledge and unconditional love that reside within the higher realms. By cultivating a deep sense of presence and surrender, we can align ourselves with the divine guidance that flows effortlessly through our lives.

To receive divine guidance, it is essential to create a sacred space within ourselves. This can be achieved through daily meditation, prayer, or contemplation. By stilling the mind and connecting with the essence of our being, we create a space for divine inspiration to enter our lives. It is important to cultivate patience and trust in the process, allowing the answers and guidance to unfold naturally and effortlessly.

Guided visualization and meditation are powerful tools for connecting with higher consciousness. These practices can transport us beyond the limitations of our physical reality and into the realm of spiritual enlightenment. By quieting the mind and focusing our attention inward, we can access deep states of relaxation and enter into a state of expanded awareness.

One effective technique is to visualize a staircase leading upwards. As we ascend each step, we release any attachments or limitations that hold us back from experiencing higher realms of consciousness. With each step, we become more attuned to the divine vibrations that surround us, allowing us to connect with higher consciousness. Visualization exercises like this can be complemented with deep breathing techniques and affirmations to enhance the overall experience.

Another practice that can facilitate connection with higher consciousness is mantra meditation. By repeating a sacred mantra, such as Om or AUM, we align our vibrations with the universal energy, thereby establishing a strong connection with higher realms. This practice helps to quiet the mind, promote inner stillness, and open ourselves up to profound spiritual experiences.

Communing with the Divine through Meditation

Exploring the concept of divine communion and experiencing unity with the divine is a profound and deeply personal journey. It is a process of connecting with something greater than ourselves and experiencing a sense of oneness and interconnectedness with the universe. Through this communion with the divine, we can tap into the unlimited wisdom, love, and guidance that is available to us.

One of the most effective ways to commune with the divine is through meditation. Meditation allows us to quiet the mind, connect with our inner being, and open ourselves up to the divine presence. Here are some practices for surrendering to the divine presence and receiving spiritual blessings.

- Begin by finding a quiet and peaceful place where you can meditate without any distractions. Sit in a comfortable position, close your eyes, and take a few deep breaths to relax your body and calm your mind.
- Set an intention for your meditation, focusing on your desire to commune with the divine. You may choose to surrender to the divine will, seek guidance, or simply deepen your connection.
- Bring your awareness to your breath and allow yourself to become fully present in the moment. Notice the sensation of breath entering and leaving your body, letting go of any tension or thoughts that arise.
- As you continue to breathe, imagine a warm, golden light surrounding you. This light represents the divine presence and love that is always available to you. Feel this light enveloping your entire being, filling you with a sense of peace and serenity.
- Now, visualize yourself merging with this divine light, becoming one with it. Feel the boundaries between yourself and the divine melting away, as you experience a deep sense of unity and oneness.
- Allow yourself to surrender completely to the divine presence, letting go of any resistance or control. Trust that the divine is guiding and supporting you every step of the way.
- Stay in this state of communion for as long as feels comfortable to you. Trust your intuition and let the experience unfold naturally. You may receive insights, guidance, or spiritual blessings during this time.
- When you are ready, gently bring your awareness back to your physical body. Take a few deep breaths, wiggle your fingers and toes, and slowly open your eyes. Take a moment to honor and acknowledge the divine presence within and around you.

These guided meditations and visualizations can deepen your connection with the divine through meditation. Remember, the key is to approach these practices with an open heart and a willingness to surrender. Trust that the divine is always there, ready to commune with you, and embrace the blessings and wisdom that come from this sacred connection.

Mindfulness in Different Cultures

Mindfulness Practices in Eastern Traditions

Exploring Mindfulness Practices in Eastern Traditions

Eastern traditions, such as Buddhism, Hinduism, and other ancient spiritual practices, have long embraced mindfulness as a core component of spiritual development. In this section, we will delve into the rich and diverse mindfulness practices found within these traditions, exploring their origins, philosophies, and techniques.

Discussing the Cultural and Philosophical Underpinnings of Eastern Mindfulness Practices

Meditation and mindfulness practices in Eastern traditions are deeply rooted in the culture and philosophies of their respective societies. Understanding these underpinnings can shed light on the purpose and significance of mindfulness in these traditions. From the Buddhist concept of impermanence and non-attachment to the Hindu idea of interconnectedness, these philosophies shape the way mindfulness is approached and practiced. This section will provide an exploration of these cultural and philosophical foundations.

Exploring Variations and Adaptations of Mindfulness Practices in Different Eastern Cultures

While mindfulness practices share common threads across Eastern traditions, they also exhibit variations and adaptations unique to different cultures. This section will take a closer look at how mindfulness practices have evolved in various Eastern cultures, including China, Japan, Tibet, and Thailand. We will explore techniques such as walking meditation, tea ceremony, and a wide range of mindfulness rituals that have been developed and passed down through the generations.

Mindful Living in Western Societies

Mindful Living in Western Societies

As mindfulness practices continue to gain popularity, more and more individuals in Western societies are embracing the concept of mindful living. The integration and adoption of mindfulness in these societies have brought about numerous benefits and have paved the way for a shift towards a more present and conscious way of life.

One of the key reasons for the rise of mindfulness in Western societies is its ability to combat the stress and pressures of modern life. As individuals navigate through the fast-paced and demanding nature of Western culture, the practice of mindfulness offers a much-needed pause. By incorporating mindfulness into their daily routines, individuals can cultivate a sense of calm and clarity, allowing them to navigate through challenges with greater ease.

Furthermore, mindful living has become increasingly popular among those who identify with the spiritual and new age movements. For these individuals, mindfulness serves as a pathway to self-discovery and personal growth. By turning inward and cultivating a greater sense of self-awareness, practitioners are able to connect with their inner wisdom and intuition, leading to a more authentic and fulfilling life.

Mindful living in Western societies also extends beyond the individual level, impacting various aspects of society as a whole. The workplace, for example, has seen a shift towards incorporating mindfulness practices to enhance employee well-being and performance. Many companies now offer mindfulness programs and encourage employees to take regular breaks to practice meditation and stress-reduction techniques.

In addition, the education system in Western societies has recognized the benefits of mindfulness for students. Schools are now incorporating mindfulness practices into the curriculum, helping students develop emotional regulation skills, improve concentration, and foster a positive and inclusive classroom environment.

Despite the numerous benefits and the growing popularity of mindful living, there are also challenges that arise when integrating mindfulness into Western contexts. One challenge is the commercialization and commodification of mindfulness, with some seeing it as a trendy or superficial practice. However, it is important to remember that at its core, mindfulness is a profound and transformative practice that goes beyond its superficial portrayal.

Another challenge is the cultural adaptation required when practicing mindfulness in Western societies. Mindfulness originated from Eastern philosophical and religious traditions, and some argue that its essence may be lost or diluted when transplanted into a Western cultural context. It is crucial to approach mindfulness with respect and understanding of its cultural roots while adapting it to meet the needs and values of Western societies.

In conclusion, mindful living has gained significant traction in Western societies as individuals seek refuge from the stresses of modern life, and as spiritual and new age movements continue to grow. Mindfulness offers a way to cultivate present moment awareness, personal growth, and overall well-being. However, the integration of mindfulness in Western contexts also presents challenges related to commercialization and cultural adaptation. It is important to approach mindfulness with respect and authenticity to fully reap its benefits in Western societies.

Cultural Perspectives on Meditation

In cultures around the world, meditation plays a significant role in spiritual traditions. It is important to note that different cultures have unique perspectives on meditation, and it can take various forms depending on the specific spiritual beliefs and practices of a community.

For example, in traditional Hindu culture, meditation is often seen as a means to connect with the divine. Practitioners may engage in mantra meditation, where a specific word or sound is repeated, or they may focus on visualizations to enter a deep state of concentration. The goal is to achieve a state of oneness with the universe and ultimately reach enlightenment.

In Buddhist culture, meditation is an essential part of the spiritual path. There are various techniques, such as mindfulness meditation, where one focuses on the present moment and observes the thoughts and sensations without judgment. Zen meditation, on the other hand, emphasizes sitting in stillness and emptying the mind. These practices aim to cultivate awareness, wisdom, and compassion.

Many cultures have developed their own unique meditation practices and techniques, each with its own purpose and focus. Let's explore a few of them:

In Japanese culture, there is a form of meditation called Zazen, which translates to sitting meditation. It is commonly practiced in Zen Buddhism and involves sitting in a specific posture, focusing on the breath, and observing the mind without getting attached to thoughts or emotions. This practice aims to cultivate stillness and awareness.

In Tibetan Buddhism, practitioners engage in a form of meditation known as Tonglen, which means giving and taking. During this practice, individuals visualize taking in the suffering of others and sending them love, compassion, and healing. It is believed to develop empathy and generate positive energy.

In Indigenous cultures, meditation takes on different forms. For example, Native American traditions often incorporate drumming and chanting as a way to enter a trance-like state and connect with the spirit world. Australian Aboriginal cultures use dadirri, a form of deep listening and stillness, to connect with the land and gain spiritual insights.

While there are diverse practices and techniques of meditation across different cultures, there are also common threads and universal principles that underlie these practices:

One such principle is the cultivation of mindfulness or present moment awareness. In many cultures, meditation is seen as a way to develop heightened awareness and attention to the present moment. This quality of mindfulness can lead to a deeper understanding of oneself and the world around us.

Another common thread is the intention to cultivate inner peace and well-being. Regardless of the specific technique or form of meditation, the ultimate goal is often to find inner harmony, reduce stress, and experience a sense of inner calm and tranquility.

Additonally, many cultures emphasize the transformative potential of meditation. It is seen as a tool for personal growth, self-discovery, and spiritual awakening. Through regular meditation practice, individuals can tap into their inner wisdom and uncover their true nature.

The study of cultural perspectives on meditation provides a rich tapestry of practices and beliefs that highlight the vast and diverse human experience. By exploring these different perspectives, we can deepen our understanding of the universal pursuit of spiritual growth and self-realization.

The Role of Mindfulness in Yoga

Integrating Mindfulness into Yoga

Yoga is a practice that has been around for thousands of years, originating in ancient India. It combines physical postures, breath control, and meditation to promote overall well-being and spiritual growth. In recent years, there has been a growing interest in the integration of mindfulness practices into the practice of yoga. Mindfulness, a concept derived from Buddhist meditation techniques, involves bringing one's attention to the present moment without judgment.

Integrating mindfulness into yoga can enhance the benefits of the practice, helping individuals to cultivate a deeper sense of awareness and presence both on and off the mat. By incorporating mindfulness techniques such as focused breathing and body scanning, yogis can develop a greater sense of connection with their bodies, thoughts, and emotions.

Mindfulness is particularly important in yoga postures, also known as asanas. By practicing present-moment awareness during asanas, individuals can deepen their experience and understanding of the postures. This involves paying attention to sensations in the body, observing the breath, and noticing any thoughts or emotions that arise. Through this heightened awareness, yogis can gain insights into their physical and mental states, allowing for a more holistic and integrated practice.

The integration of mindfulness in yoga can also extend to the energetic aspects of the practice. In yoga, it is believed that there is a subtle energy system called the pranic body, which consists of nadis (energy channels) and chakras (energy centers). Mindfulness can help individuals to cultivate a deeper sense of connection with their energetic body and develop an awareness of the flow of prana (life force energy) within them.

By incorporating mindfulness practices such as breath awareness, visualization, and mantra repetition, yogis can enhance their energetic experience during yoga practice. This can lead to a greater sense of balance, harmony, and vitality in both the physical and energetic bodies.

Overall, the integration of mindfulness practices into the practice of yoga can deepen one's experience and understanding of the practice. It allows for a deeper sense of connection with the present moment, the body, and the subtle aspects of the practice. Whether you are new to yoga or have been practicing for years, exploring mindfulness in your yoga practice can have profound benefits for your overall well-being and spiritual growth.

Yogic Breathing and Meditation

Breath is a fundamental aspect of the yogic tradition, connecting the mind, body, and spirit. In yoga, breath is considered a manifestation of prana, the life force energy that flows through all living beings. By harnessing the power of breath through meditation, we can explore the depths of our consciousness and experience a profound sense of inner peace and clarity.

Pranayama, the practice of yogic breathing techniques, plays a vital role in deepening the meditation experience. These techniques involve consciously manipulating the breath to refine and direct the flow of prana in the body. By focusing on breath awareness and control, we can calm the mind, improve concentration, and unlock the dormant potential within us.

There are various types of pranayama, each with its own unique effects on the mind and body. One such technique is Anulom Vilom or alternate nostril breathing. This practice involves inhaling and exhaling through one nostril at a time, alternating between the left and right nostrils. Anulom Vilom harmonizes the energies in the body, purifies the nadis (energy channels), and brings balance and harmony to the mind.

Another popular pranayama technique is Sitali Pranayama or the cooling breath. This technique involves curling the tongue and inhaling deeply through the rolled tongue, creating a cooling sensation in the body. Sitali Pranayama helps to calm the nervous system, reduce stress and anxiety, and bring a sense of refreshment and rejuvenation.

One of the most powerful pranayama practices is Kapalabhati or the skull-shining breath. This technique involves forceful exhalations followed by passive inhalations, rapidly pumping the belly. Kapalabhati increases the flow of oxygen in the body, cleanses the respiratory system, and energizes the mind. It is also known to enhance mental clarity and focus.

Now that we have explored some of the yogic breathing techniques, let us move on to guided breathing and meditation practices that can enhance mindfulness and deepen the yoga experience. One such practice is Mindful Breathing Meditation. In this practice, we focus our attention solely on the breath, observing its sensations as it enters and leaves the body. By anchoring our awareness to the breath, we cultivate present-moment awareness and develop a state of deep relaxation and inner stillness.

Another powerful practice is Loving-Kindness Meditation or Metta Bhavana. This meditation involves silently repeating phrases of love, kindness, and compassion towards oneself and others. By combining the breath with heartfelt intentions, we can cultivate feelings of love, compassion, and connection towards ourselves and all beings.

It is important to remember that the breath is our constant companion and a gateway to our inner world. By incorporating pranayama and meditation into our yoga practice, we can harness the power of breath, deepen our connection to prana, and experience profound transformation on all levels of our being.

Mindfulness in Yoga Philosophy

Yoga philosophy goes far beyond physical exercise; it encompasses a rich tradition of mind-body practices aimed at achieving self-realization and spiritual growth. Central to this philosophy is the concept of mindfulness, which plays a crucial role in the practice of yoga. In this subchapter, we will explore the significance and application of mindfulness in the context of yoga philosophy.

Mindfulness, in the context of yoga philosophy, refers to the state of being fully present in the present moment, without judgment or attachment. It involves cultivating awareness of one's thoughts, emotions, and physical sensations, as well as the environment and interactions with others. Through mindfulness, practitioners aim to develop a deeper understanding of themselves and their place in the world.

One of the key aspects of mindfulness in yoga philosophy is its focus on the here and now. Yogic teachings emphasize the importance of living in the present moment, rather than dwelling on the past or worrying about the future. By cultivating mindfulness, practitioners learn to fully immerse themselves in their experiences, enhancing their sense of gratitude, joy, and inner peace.

Another fundamental concept in yoga philosophy is the principle of non-attachment. Non-attachment refers to the ability to let go of attachments to outcomes, desires, and material possessions. It involves detaching oneself from the ego and embracing a mindset of acceptance and surrender. Mindfulness plays a crucial role in developing non-attachment, as it allows practitioners to observe their thoughts and emotions without getting caught up in them.

The integration of mindfulness in the study and application of yoga philosophy is essential for deepening one's spiritual journey. By practicing mindfulness on and off the mat, practitioners can cultivate greater self-awareness, compassion, and resilience. Mindfulness also serves as a tool for managing stress, anxiety, and other mental and emotional challenges, helping individuals navigate the ups and downs of life with greater ease.

In conclusion, mindfulness is an integral part of yoga philosophy, contributing to self-realization and spiritual growth. By cultivating mindfulness, practitioners can deepen their understanding of themselves and the world around them, while developing valuable skills for navigating life's challenges. The practice of mindfulness in yoga philosophy offers a path to greater inner peace, joy, and fulfillment.

Building a Meditation Practice

Establishing a Regular Meditation Routine

Establishing a Regular Meditation Routine

Consistency and commitment are key when it comes to establishing a regular meditation practice. By dedicating yourself to a daily meditation routine, you can experience profound benefits for your spiritual well-being.

To start, it's important to create a conducive environment for your meditation practice. Find a quiet and comfortable space where you won't be easily distracted. This could be a corner of your home or a designated meditation area. Make sure the area is clean and free from any clutter.

In addition to the physical environment, it's important to set realistic goals for your meditation practice. Start with a manageable amount of time, such as 5 or 10 minutes, and gradually increase the duration as you become more comfortable. Remember, the goal is consistency, so choose a duration that you can commit to on a daily basis.

Before you begin your meditation, it can be helpful to establish a routine. Set a specific time each day for your practice, whether it's in the morning, before bed, or during a lunch break. By creating a routine, you signal to your mind and body that meditation is a priority.

Now that you have set the stage for your meditation practice, it's time to dive into the actual technique. There are various types of meditation practices, so it's important to find one that resonates with you. Some popular options include mindfulness meditation, loving-kindness meditation, and transcendental meditation.

Regardless of the technique you choose, it's important to start with the basics. Find a comfortable seated position, keeping your spine straight and relaxed. Close your eyes or soften your gaze, and begin to bring your attention to your breath. Notice the sensation of the breath as it enters and leaves your body.

As thoughts or distractions arise, gently bring your focus back to the breath. Don't judge or criticize yourself for getting distracted; simply acknowledge the thought and return to your breath. Remember, meditation is about cultivating a non-judgmental awareness of the present moment.

Consistency is key when it comes to developing a regular meditation practice. Aim for daily practice, even if it's just for a few minutes. Over time, you will start to notice the benefits of meditation in your daily life, including increased clarity, decreased stress, and a greater sense of inner peace.

Keep in mind that meditation is a personal journey, and what works for one person may not work for another. Be open to exploring different techniques and finding what resonates with you. With consistency, commitment, and an open mind, you can establish a fulfilling and transformative meditation practice.

Overcoming Challenges in Meditation

Meditation is a powerful practice for cultivating mindfulness and inner peace. However, it can be challenging at times, especially for those who are new to the spiritual journey. In this subchapter, we will explore some common challenges that arise during meditation and provide techniques to overcome them. Through these strategies, you will be able to deepen your meditation practice and experience its profound benefits.

Addressing common challenges and obstacles in meditation:

Meditation can sometimes bring restlessness or a lack of focus. It is important to remember that restlessness is a natural part of the mind's process of settling. When restlessness arises, acknowledge it without judgment and gently bring your attention back to your breath or chosen meditation object.

Another challenge is a lack of focus. To cultivate focus, start with short meditation sessions and gradually increase the duration. It may also be helpful to choose a single-pointed focus, such as counting the breath or repeating a mantra. If the mind wanders, gently guide your attention back to the chosen focus.

Discussing techniques for dealing with distractions, physical discomfort, and resistance:

Distractions are a common hindrance during meditation. Rather than fighting against them, acknowledge their presence and let them pass without attachment or judgment. You can also try using ambient sounds or soft music to create a peaceful environment.

Physical discomfort is another challenge that may arise. Ensure that you are sitting in a comfortable position, either on a chair or on a cushion. Adjust your posture as needed to alleviate any discomfort. If necessary, you can also incorporate gentle movement or stretching before your meditation session.

Resistance is a natural defense mechanism of the mind. When resistance arises, explore it with curiosity and compassion. Understand that resistance is often a sign of growth and transformation. By allowing yourself to fully experience and embrace resistance, you can transcend its limitations and move forward on your spiritual path.

Providing guidance and support for maintaining motivation and overcoming meditation roadblocks:

One common roadblock is a lack of motivation. It can be helpful to set realistic goals and create a consistent meditation routine. Remember to celebrate small victories and acknowledge the progress you are making. Connecting with a meditation community or finding a meditation buddy can also help to boost motivation.

Another roadblock is the feeling of being stuck or not making progress in your meditation practice. If you find yourself in this situation, it can be beneficial to explore different meditation techniques or seek guidance from a qualified meditation teacher. Remember that progress in meditation is not always linear, and each meditation session is an opportunity for growth.

By overcoming challenges in meditation, you can deepen your practice and reap the many benefits it has to offer. Stay committed, be gentle with yourself, and trust in the transformative power of meditation.

Creating a Sacred Space for Meditation

Creating a Sacred Space for Meditation

Exploring the importance of creating a dedicated and sacred space for meditation:

In the realm of spirituality and personal growth, having a dedicated space for meditation is essential. This space serves as a sanctuary, a place where you can escape the distractions of the outside world and focus on your inner self. By designating a specific area solely for your meditation practice, you create a sense of intention and reverence. This sacred space becomes a refuge, where you can connect with your spiritual essence and find peace amidst the chaos of everyday life.

Discussing the role of rituals, symbols, and intentional objects in enhancing the meditation experience:

Rituals, symbols, and intentional objects play a significant role in enhancing the meditation experience within your sacred space. Rituals add a sense of ceremony and structure to your practice. Whether it's lighting a candle, burning incense, or reciting a specific mantra, these rituals can act as powerful anchors that signal your mind and body to enter a meditative state. Symbols, such as statues or images of spiritual figures, can serve as focal points, creating a visual representation of the qualities you seek to cultivate in your meditation. Intentional objects, such as crystals, feathers, or artwork, can hold personal significance and act as reminders of your intentions and aspirations. Integrating these elements into your sacred space can deepen your connection to the practice and enhance its transformative power.

Guidance for creating a personalized sacred space that supports focus, relaxation, and inner peace:

Creating a personalized sacred space is an opportunity to infuse your meditation practice with your unique energy and intentions. Here are some practical tips to help you design a space that supports your focus, relaxation, and inner peace:

1. Find a quiet and comfortable location: Choose a space where you can retreat from external distractions. It could be a corner of a room, a spare room, or even a designated area in your backyard.

2. Clear the space energetically: Before setting up your sacred space, cleanse the area to remove any negative or stagnant energies. You can use smudging tools like sage or palo santo, or simply visualize a purification of the space with white light.

3. Set the mood with lighting: Lighting plays a crucial role in creating a serene atmosphere. Opt for soft, diffused lighting, such as candles or Himalayan salt lamps, to induce a sense of calmness and tranquility.

4. Integrate natural elements: Bring the healing energy of nature into your sacred space by incorporating natural elements. Consider adding plants, flowers, or a small water feature to create a sense of harmony and connection with the Earth.

5. Choose meaningful objects: Select objects that hold personal significance and resonate with your spiritual journey. It could be a favorite crystal, a spiritual text, or a piece of art that inspires you. These objects will serve as focal points for your meditation practice.

6. Create a comfortable seating arrangement: Invest in a comfortable meditation cushion or chair that supports an upright and relaxed posture. The physical comfort of your body is crucial for deepening your meditation practice.

7. Establish a sense of privacy: If possible, create a sense of privacy in your sacred space. You can use curtains, screens, or even room dividers to separate the area from daily distractions. This will allow you to fully immerse yourself in your meditation practice.

8. Personalize with intention: Finally, infuse your sacred space with your personal intention. Whether it's cultivating mindfulness, inner peace, or spiritual growth, remind yourself of your purpose each time you enter your sacred space. This intentional focus will deepen your practice and create a sacred container for your inner exploration.

Author: Mike Davidson

Mike Davidson is a new writer wishing to add his contributions to the rise of the new earth, raising vibration and general wellbeing to the populous. An understanding of fifteen years of spiritual studying, incorporating mindfulness and some studies on awakening the third eye, Mike brings a unique perspective to his writing, bringing un understanding of the subject to the masses with the dawn of a new earth on the horizon.

Background:

Mike was born and raised in the Scottish Borders originally coming from the City of Stirling, Although Mike was brought up in the Borders of Scotland, he has never forgotten his roots. Mike was a successful chef of twenty-eight years in the hotel/catering trade, now later on in life, with three beautiful daughters (Edith, Heather and Paige) and a failed marriage.

Mike looked deep inside of himself. Although, not religious, Mike had a calling to the spiritual side of life, taking a look at the bigger picture and trying to understand our auric energies and the universe in this ever-maddening world we all live in.

About the Book:

Mindfulness, Meditation and opening the third eye.

Overview:

This book is designed to be a self-help guide of sorts to help those of whom would like to see a calmer side of themselves, steering away from the madness of our world and surroundings.

Printed in Great Britain
by Amazon

42343772R00036